The Shoes of Salvation

you know who you are

07 08 09 10 11 SDB 10 9 8 7 6 5 4 3 2 1

ISBN-13: 978-0-7407-6867-5
ISBN-10: 0-7407-6867-0

www.edwardmonkton.com

www.andrewsmcmeel.com

ATTENTION: SCHOOLS AND BUSINESSES

Andrews McMeel books are available at quantity discounts
with bulk purchase for educational, business, or sales promo-
tional use. For information, please write to: Special Sales
Department, Andrews McMeel Publishing, LLC, 4520 Main
Street, Kansas City, Missouri 64111.

The SHOES of SALVATION

Edward Monkton

**Andrews McMeel
Publishing, LLC**

Kansas City

There was once a
LADY.

Even though the lady
was not RICH, she was
not POOR either.

And even though she was beset by the small NUISANCES of everyday life, she was CONTENT enough.

But the lady could not help feeling that there was something MISSING.

There was a hollowness, an EMPTINESS in her that needed to be FILLED.

She knew that out there, SOMEWHERE, was something that could CHANGE her life completely.

Make her WHOLE.
Give her MEANING.

Perhaps
a MAN...

a JOURNEY...

a spiritual
AWAKENING...

a holy and
mysterious
CALLING...

and then she saw
**THE BEAUTIFUL
SHOES**
and she knew that
they were all she needed.

"Come to us, lady," said the shoes, "and we will make you BEAUTIFUL too.

"We alone can make you blossom and flourish into a glorious and whole and COMPLETE Human Being."

"But you are so EXPENSIVE,"
said the lady. "I cannot
possibly afford you."

"Look at our beautiful
STRAPS," said the shoes.
"Look at our wonderful
SHINY leather. Look at
the turn of our heels and
the shape of our toes.

"Do you think we should be cheaper? Do you think everyone should be able to AFFORD the happiness, the pleasure, the ECSTASY that we can offer?"

"You are right," said the lady. "I am sorry that I ever doubted you. Please FORGIVE me."

So the lady gave the shopkeeper ALL the MONEY she had and she walked away with the BEAUTIFUL shoes.

When the lady got home, she tried on the shoes. Instantly, they began to **PINCH** and to **HURT** the lady's feet terribly.

"Oh, shoes," said the lady, "I thought you would bring me **ECSTASY**, but all I can feel is **PAIN!**"

"Oh, lady," said the shoes, "the pain we GIVE you is simply to remind you of our PRESENCE. Do you not want it to be constantly in your mind that we are here on your feet, making you WONDERFUL, making you GLORIOUS, causing you to shine and to DAZZLE?"

"You are right again," said
the lady. "Thank you, Shoes."

That evening, the lady wore the BEAUTIFUL shoes to a cocktail party.

Despite the AGONY and the terrible price of the shoes, the lady knew that she felt better than any man or journey or holy and MYSTERIOUS calling could possibly ever make her feel.

For the first time in her
life, the lady felt COMPLETE.

And the lady knew what she had INSTINCTIVELY known all along.

That sometimes, only GLORIOUS SHOES can SAVE you.

THE END